Career Development and the Future of Work:
A Conversation Guide
SECOND EDITION

Written by Lisa Taylor, Challenge Factory

Co-Created with Jennifer La Trobe and Tim Caswell, Creative Connection

Copyright © 2020 Challenge Factory Inc.

720 Bathurst Street
Toronto, ON M5S 2R4
Canada

www.challengefactory.ca
clientsupport@challengefactory.ca

ISBN
Paperback: 978-1-7772284-2-2

Author: Lisa Taylor
Co-Creators: Jennifer La Trobe and Tim Caswell
Design and Layout: Jacqui Burke

Photos: Creative Connection

No part of this publication may be reproduced, distributed, or transmitted in any form or by any means, including photocopying, recording or other electronic or mechanical methods, without the prior written permission of the publisher, except in the case of brief quotations embodied in critical reviews and certain other non-commercial uses permitted by copyright law. Every reasonable effort has been made to identify the owners of copyright material reproduced in this publication and to comply with Canadian Copyright law. The publisher would welcome any information regarding errors or omissions. Wholesale discounts for book orders are available through Ingram Distributors.

Table of Contents

Acknowledgments 1

About Challenge Factory 2

Why a Conversation Guide? 3

    You and Your Team Can Change the World 4

A Note to Facilitators 5

A Note to Participants 9

Future of Work Conversations 10

    Conversation A

        To Dread and to Dream the Future of Work 10

    Conversation B

        The Intersection of our Sector and the Future of Work 14

    Conversation C

        Taking Action to Shape the Future of Work 18

Appendix 23

    Worksheets 23

    Additional Resources 32

Acknowledgments

I would like to acknowledge the financial support that the first edition of this project received from the Ontario Centre for Workforce Innovation, Ryerson University, and the Ontario Ministry of Advanced Education and Skills Development.

This *Guide* is informed by discussions that took place with delegates at Cannexus18, a bilingual Canadian conference organized by CERIC that focuses on career development. I am grateful for Riz Ibrahim and Danielle Levitt's support and assistance not just on-site, but also in taking a leap of faith that a meaningful 1000+ person conversation could be accomplished alongside a busy conference agenda.

In addition to the more than one thousand delegates at Cannexus18, this project was strengthened by feedback received in a focus group held in Toronto in March 2018. We appreciate the time and thoughtfulness of our attendees: Connie Tang, Amanda Channon, Melissa Wilson, Kyle Walker, Jonathan Coulman, Mark Venning, Haris Blentic, Marianne Moore, Nancy McGarvie, Solomon Yun, and Marie Heron.

Since 2018, more than 3,000 Canadians have contributed to the ongoing conversation on the Future of Work—and over that time, members of the Challenge Factory team have supported this project's many moving parts. I thank Andrew Marchant (PMP), Chris Martin, Cayla Charles, Nev Balendra, Taryn Blanchard and Jacqui Burke.

This was my first experience creating a film and I am grateful for the talent, creativity, and patience of Michael Lobel, a talented filmmaker with a clear passion for stories that create a better world.

I could not have wished for better co-creators and collaborators than Jennifer La Trobe and Tim Casswell of Creative Connection. Together, they are an unparalleled team brimming with vision, commitment, passion, and a talent for challenging leaders and organizations to dream into a future based on intention. Their strategic and creative support for this project has been absolute and I'm grateful for the friendship that has grown out of our intense work together. Thanks to Mark Bowden and Tracey Thompson for introducing Jeni and I years ago. You were right in thinking we should know each other.

Finally, a word of appreciation and admiration for the career development, employment services, and human resource professionals across Canada, whose work with individuals and employers in academic institutions, community organizations, indigenous organizations, non-profits and charities, and faith communities ensure stronger future employment prospects for everyone, including those who are most vulnerable.

Lisa Taylor, President
Challenge Factory

About Challenge Factory

Since our founding in 2011, Challenge Factory has been tracking the changes that are taking place in the world of work. We believe that everyone should meet these changes head on by taking control of their own future. Our systems-focused consulting, research, and learning services provide creative yet practical solutions to today's most pressing career and workforce challenges. We serve clients from a range of corporate, institutional, and government sectors—offering proven methodologies, expertise, and experience. Together, we shape the Future of Work.

For more information, please visit www.challengefactory.ca.

Challenge Factory publications:

The Talent Revolution: Longevity and the Future of Work (Lisa Taylor and Fern Lebo)

The Canadian Guide to Hiring Veterans (Coming Fall 2020)

Retain and Gain Playbook Series:
- Career Management for Small Business
- Career Management for Nonprofits and Charities
- Career Management for the Public Sector (Coming 2021)

Why a Conversation Guide?

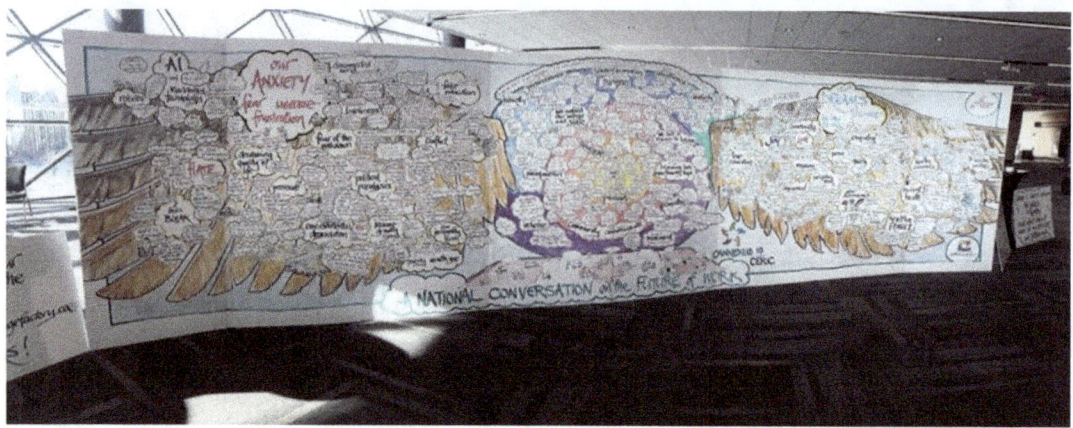

Change is happening. It was happening long before the COVID-19 pandemic disrupted our lives so quickly and dramatically. Careers, workforces, workplaces, labour markets, and all the conditions that affect them are facing challenges and opportunities—in both short- and long-term timeframes.

The past few years have seen the "Future of Work" take on a new sense of urgency and 'trendiness' across sectors, as well as in mainstream public discourse. Every day, new predictions, opinions, and decisions are being formed about *how work is going to change* and *what work is going to become*.

These types of discussions often explore the ways that technologies like automation, robotics, and artificial intelligence are impacting how we work, where we work, and the skills that we need to work. This is an important and dynamic topic, and certainly an integral part of the Future of Work. But equally important is the human side of these discussions. Equally important are questions about how the application of *human* energy, effort, and creativity are impacting our work, work environments, and skillsets.

The Future of Work is human. It's you, your clients, and your funders. As such, this *Conversation Guide* is designed to put humans, rather than technology, in the driver's seat.

You and Your Team Can Change the World

This *Conversation Guide* will lead you and your team through a series of activities that challenge you to participate in the creation of a collective future. There is a wealth of experience, case studies, and wisdom in the career development and employment services sector. This body of knowledge and expertise urgently needs to be part of the ongoing conversation about the Future of Work. And so we invite you—leaders, team members, activators, and trailblazers—to take up a pivotal role in developing, synthesizing, and implementing the ideas that will shape the Future of Work.

Together, let's get started.

"Never doubt that a small group of thoughtful, committed, citizens can change the world. Indeed, it is the only thing that ever has."
– Margaret Mead

A Note to Facilitators

You have everything you need to facilitate a timely and much needed conversation about the Future of Work in your workplace. This *Guide*—along with its companion video—will help you create an engaging, energized, and safe environment for all members of your team to participate.

It's crucial that as many voices and perspectives as possible are involved in this conversation. This includes team members with different roles and positions within your organization, as well as at different stages in their own careers. Don't leave anyone behind and make it a priority to hear from everyone.

Constructive conversations require mindful preparation. Use the following three activities to prepare both yourself, your team members, and your work environment.

Materials and equipment to bring to the conversation

- ✓ Flipchart paper
- ✓ Tape
- ✓ Markers
- ✓ Post-it notes
- ✓ Link to video*
- ✓ Copies of this *Guide*
- ✓ Laptop
- ✓ Projector
- ✓ Speakers

*https://challengefactory.ca/services/research/future-of-work/

Do you like this *Conversation Guide* but don't want to facilitate?

Challenge Factory is happy to facilitate this important conversation for your team—either online or in person. Get in touch at clientsupport@challengefactory.ca if you would like to explore this option.

Five factors to consider as you prepare for the conversation

Invitation:
What relationship do you want to establish? What tone do you want to set? How much notice do you need to give?

Make sure to emphasize that the team members being invited to the conversation are important contributors with valued viewpoints. If appropriate, recognize that this may not be the first time they've engaged in conversations about the future and they may be experiencing fatigue—but this moment is different and special. It's an opportunity you all need to grasp together, and it will be impactful.

Environment:
Think about the setting in which the conversation will take place. Will the space's set-up and lighting encourage open dialogue and a collaborative relationship?

Depending on the number of participants, sit at a round table or create a semi-circle of small tables so that team members can have discussions in smaller groups before turning to become a larger group. It's important for everyone to be able to see and engage with each other.

Pace and Timing:
How much time do you want different parts of the conversation to take? How relaxed or rigid do you want to structure the flow of discussion and activities?

Consider setting shorter, brisk time blocks for written responses, and developing a more relaxed atmosphere for activities that are focused on discussion and reflection.

Preparation:
What do you need to do to prepare as a facilitator? What do you want the participants to know in advance?

Make sure you enter the conversation feeling ready, whatever that entails for you. Emphasize that you're hoping participants will enter the conversation with genuine curiosity. That's likely all they really need to come prepared.

Flexibility:
How will you react if the conversation runs long but remains engaging?

Consider allowing the participants to decide as a group if they're willing to run longer.

Five behaviours to build into the conversation

Consider presenting this framework to participants at the beginning of your conversation. It's important to set the right tone and expectations for the activities and discussions to come.

Inviting:
Ensure an inclusive approach to the conversation that allows everyone to participate while honouring different experiences, perspectives, and personality styles.

Listening:
Actively hear what is and is not said when each participant is speaking.

Curating:
Focus on how ideas build off each other and create themes across the conversation (i.e., look for patterns, trends, and themes).

Challenging:
Ask participants to explore their beliefs, to bust myths, and to consider new paradigms.

Inspiring:
Maintain an environment that encourages honest expression of frustration, fear, and dreams (i.e., embrace both possibility and uncertainty).

How to Modify these Instructions for Remote Delivery

The first edition of this *Guide* was revised during COVID-19 times, when many work interactions shifted from offices to remote communication platforms. With a few modifications, the activities and discussions facilitated in this *Conversation Guide* can absolutely take place online.

1. The activities and discussions in this *Guide* are not for strangers. Participants need to know and trust each other if they're going to try to tackle "the big questions" about the future, themselves, and their work. There are tried-and-true methods of ensuring comfortable engagement and full participation in person. When facilitating online, however, these methods may be more difficult with a group that hasn't yet established trust. Consider how you can build team trust before using this *Guide*.

2. Some of the activities in this *Guide* use post-it notes. For an online conversation, instead set up a shared Google document and have participants add their "post-it note" comments to it directly. Assign a technically savvy and/or creative team member to be responsible for any in-document organizing or editing that is instructed during the activities.

3. Don't want to use a shared Google document? Challenge Factory can set up an online survey for your team that includes all the questions you will pose throughout this conversation. Contact us at clientsupport@challengefactory.ca for this support.

4. If your organization uses a direct messaging service, such as Slack or Facebook Workplace, set up a dedicated group or chat for participants to make comments, ask questions, and encourage one another throughout this conversation.

A Note to Participants

We can't do it alone. The future belongs to us all—and will affect us all.

We want you to be part of a conversation about the Future of Work and lifelong career development. Mindsets, models, structures, and behaviours all need to be challenged as conditions in both our workplaces and personal lives change. For example, the COVID-19 pandemic saw everyone's work and home lives run up against each other in new ways, and brought changes—for today and tomorrow—to the forefront of our minds with a new urgency. By engaging and imagining the rapidly approaching future together, we can make sure it arrives with positive and meaningful change.

Career development and employment services practitioners are not secondary players in this conversation. We're specialists in the world of work and all its many facets. We're on the frontlines of shifting labour markets, population change, talent and skills development, and education and careers. We see clients who face barriers and others who create barriers for themselves. Ours is a field ripe with methodologies—templates, research, tools, collaboration, and expertise—designed to make sense of the complex relationships between work, self, and a thriving society. Importantly, this knowledge and experience is also incredibly valuable to policymakers as they create the very programs that fund and support our work.

This *Guide* is the result of Challenge Factory's ongoing dialogue with colleagues, clients, and Canadians across the country on the Future of Work. It challenges us all to consider what matters most to us, who we want to be, what we want our society to look like in the coming years, and the best ways to make sure our voices are heard. We all have a role to play in preparing ourselves, our workplaces, and our country for employment success in a world full of uncertainty and opportunity.

Thank you for joining us on this journey.

> Note for the Facilitator
>
> If you don't plan to share this *Guide* with the participants before your session, consider including content from this section in the event invitations or a PowerPoint slide as you are making your introductory remarks.

Future of Work Conversations

One three-hour workshop or three 90-minute sessions

This section outlines three conversations that facilitate a distinct set of activities and discussions about the Future of Work. They can take place as part of one half-day workshop, or divided into three separate sessions as a cohesive series that is delivered over a time period of your choosing. For example, consider structuring them as three "lunch and learn" sessions for your team. The three-part series should be conducted in order, as each conversation builds on the work that came before it. Remember to exhibit the artifacts created in the previous session(s) during the next conversation.

Conversation A

To Dread and to Dream the Future of Work

Estimated time allotted: 90 minutes

In today's busy workplaces, many of us don't often step back from our daily tasks to really consider how we feel about what's happening around us. Sometimes there's simply no time; our workloads are always high and our resources are frequently limited. Other times this type of reflection simply feels futile when you're only one person in a broader system or organization.

Today's the day you take that step back.

Use this conversation to embrace self-reflection as you engage with your colleagues—without feelings of pressure, isolation, or inadequacy. We can't make change without talking about it first. Let's start with what we dread and dream about the Future of Work.

Activity One: What We Dread
Estimated time allotted: Five minutes

Consider today's world of work. Think about yourself trying to succeed in it, and then think about your children and your children's children trying to succeed in it.

What attitudes, behaviours, and structures fill you with unease, anxiety, frustration, anger, or fear?

Write down each thought you have on a separate post-it note.

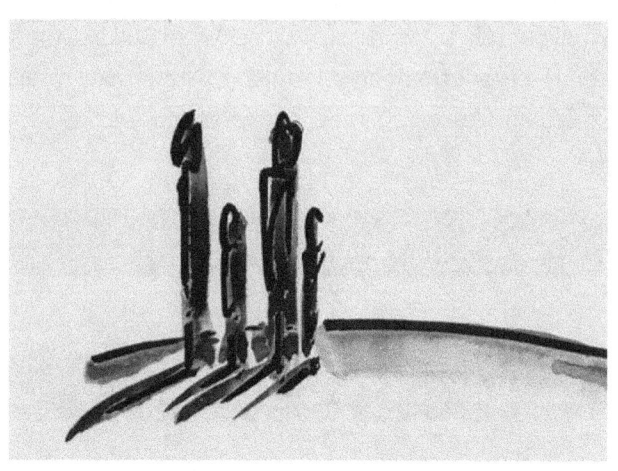

Activity Two: What We Dream
Estimated time allotted: Five minutes

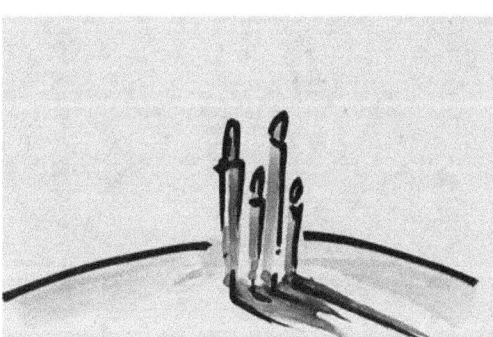

Consider the best version of the world of work that you'd like for your children and your children's children. Don't limit yourself; think creatively, imaginatively, and idealistically.

What attitudes, behaviours, and structures would that world of work have? What do you yearn for and long to see?

Activity Three: Mapping our Feelings about the Future of Work
Estimated time allotted: 30 minutes

Note for the Facilitator

Create two large flipcharts, one for each of the previous activities. Depending on the number of participants, tape more than one sheet of paper together. Have each participant, one at a time, place their post-it notes on the appropriate flipchart. If they see a post-it note that's the same as their own, have them place their post-it note on top of it. If their post-it note is similar but not exactly the same as another, have them place their own close to the original post-it. As each participant places their post-it notes on the flipcharts, have those watching take note of the common ideas, themes, keywords, and emotions that are emerging.

Give summary titles to each of the post-it clusters. Write them clearly on the flipchart.

Examine the summary of the key themes, while acknowledging that all the post-it notes are important to the conversation—even those only presented by a single member of the group. Review the whole picture that's now on the wall.

Use the following questions to generate a group discussion:

1. Which was easier for you to think of: your dreads or your dreams? Why do you think this is?
2. What themes surprised you? What's missing that you expected to see?

Add any new themes that emerge from this discussion to the flipcharts.

Activity Four: Our Colleagues Coast to Coast to Coast

Estimated time allotted: 50 minutes

Play the video (see page 5 for the URL). When it's done, give everyone one minute for silent, personal reflection before initiating discussion. Ask the participants to complete worksheet #1 (pictured below; see the Appendix for a printable version) before coming together to discuss the answers as a group. Summarize the responses on a flipchart (pictured below).

1. What are your first reactions to the video?
2. What surprised you?
3. What didn't surprise you?
4. What did the video confirm or reinforce in your current thinking?
5. How did the video change your current understanding of the following topics:
    a. Future of Work
    b. The career development and employment services sector
    c. This moment in time as it relates to your work, role, and opportunities
    d. Your personal motivation

Conversation B

The Intersection of our Sector and the Future of Work

Estimated time allotted: 90 minutes

> Note for the Facilitator
> If time has passed between Conversation A and Conversation B, ensure the room is set up with the artifacts (flipcharts, post-it notes, etc.) from Conversation A.

Activity One: The Sector's Role in the Future of Work
Estimated time allotted: 45 minutes

Play the video (see page 5 for the URL). When it's done, give everyone one minute for silent, personal reflection before initiating discussion. Ask them to consider the following three questions before sharing their answers as a group.

1. What did you see this time that you don't recall from the first time?
2. To whom would you like to show this video?
3. What effect would you like the video to have on their attitudes and actions?

Use five separate sheets of flipchart paper (pictured below) to discuss and record the following:

- Sheet #1. A short list of two or three client or population groups that you most want to see a change in, and what those changes would be.
- Sheet #2. The negative attitudes and behaviours that you currently see in the clients or population groups.
- Sheet #3. The positive attitude and behaviour that you want to see in the client or population groups.
- Sheet #4. If you believe the client or population groups are eager for change, how does this affect your attitudes and actions?
- Sheet #5. If you believe the client or population groups are unwilling to listen to you or change, how does it affect your attitudes and behaviours?

In the time remaining, discuss how you may be able to interpret the current behaviours of your target client or population groups as demonstrating *in some way* a desire and interest for meaningful change. What does this desire/interest look like for them? Why may it look different than other groups' desire/interest? We will take this further in the next exercise.

Sheet #1

Sheet #2-3

Sheet #4

Sheet #5

Activity Two: Choosing Your Workplace's Future of Work Belief System
Estimated time allocated: 45 minutes

Review the flipcharts. Review all ideas that have be contributed thus far. Recognize that our beliefs affect our attitudes and behaviours. There is power in consciously choosing, agreeing, and committing to your beliefs.

As a group, choose five beliefs that you hold to be true with respect to the Future of Work in your workplace. For example, you might agree that you will believe meaningful change is possible, or that contrary views deserve exploration.

These beliefs will be your guide. They will remind you to treat yourselves, others, and the situations that you experience in ways that encourage your best attitudes and behaviours. Focusing on your best attitudes and behaviours creates an environment in which you and your clients can engage meaningfully. It allows you to be the change that will lead to your chosen future.

Record these truths on a flipchart.

Look around the room. Who among your colleagues can help you remember these truths and live them for yourself, the people around you, and the situations you experience? Who can you help do the same?

Identify one or two colleagues and agree to act as each other's "truth-minders." Together, you will gently remind each other to "keep the faith" and hold to these truths whenever you encounter situations, relationships, or other interactions that test your patience, positivity, and stress levels. Whenever the need arises, you will refocus each other on the future that you want to shape and create in your workplace, and the truths that act as your way forward.

The rest of this activity takes place in small groups.

In groups of three, use the truths that you've recorded to identify examples from your real work experiences of the following:

1. What it looks and feels like when the truth is believed.
2. What it looks and feels like when the truth is overwhelmed, forgotten, or displaced by another truth.

For example:

1. Think of someone you know who typically has a positive, enthusiastic attitude. One day you see them displaying a negative, cynical attitude. What do you think, feel, and do?
2. Imagine someone you know who has a negative, cynical, or manipulative attitude. One day you see them acting positive and enthusiastic. What do you think, feel, and do?

Now let's try a "what if" exercise.

What if… We didn't have stressful workloads, budget concerns, or feelings of powerlessness?

Who would we be? What would we do? How would this make us feel or behave?

Your workplace and clients needs you to take on the role of changemaker, trailblazer, and activator. In small groups, discuss behaviours and actions that you may be able to take in this role.

Decide whether you want to be 1) as imaginative as possible, or 2) grounded in concrete, doable activities or goals. Both approaches are stimulating and valid methods in the context of this conversation.

Identify thought patterns and behaviours that erode your motivation in this role. Then consider ways that may help you reorient and refocus when you start to slip into these patterns and behaviours. Creating change comes with ups and downs, starts and stops, forwards and backwards progress. Acknowledge this and think of ways to get back on track during disruptions and uncertainty.

Hint: you've just identified your "truth-minder" colleagues.

Conversation C

Taking Action to Shape the Future of Work

Estimated time allotted: 90 minutes

Activity One: From Curiosity to Framework – Five Future of Work Drivers
Estimated allotted time: 60 minutes

> Note for the Facilitator
> If time has passed between Conversation B and Conversation C, ensure the room is set up with the artifacts (flipcharts, post-it notes, etc.) from Conversations A and B.

Have each participant complete the following statement on a post-it note and place it on a flipchart:

"I'm curious about what _____ may look like in the future."

Now let's "upvote" the ideas on the flipchart. Have each person pick one of the ideas on the flipchart and explain in a single sentence why it interests or concerns them.

When everyone has responded, break into small groups to discuss the ideas that have been presented. Have each group answer the following two questions:

1. What do you notice about the ideas presented?
2. What themes or categories of curiosity do you see emerging?

Come back from the small group discussion. As a single group, reorder the post-it notes on the flipchart into themes or categories, organizing similar ideas together.

Challenge Factory has identified five drivers that are shaping the Future of Work. These drivers do not define what the future will hold. Rather, they help ensure we have a comprehensive understanding of how the world of work is now and will continue to change in the future.

1. Demographics and longevity
   Who's getting ahead, and who's being left behind in the world of work? We're all living through the same times, but we experience the world of work differently depending on our age, education, socioeconomic background, gender, race, and so on.

2. Career ownership
   Who has control over your career? The relationship between employee and employer is changing, including expectations and agency surrounding career choices, advancements, opportunities, and challenges.

3. The freelance or gig economy
   Permanent, full-time job positions are giving way to shorter term contracts, informal work, and employment that may have less job security and/or more flexibility and freedom.

4. The rise of platforms
   More and more business models rely on platforms to do business, reach customers, and deliver their services (e.g., Amazon, Skip the Dishes, Uber, Upwork, etc.)

5. AI and robotics
   New technologies (big and small) are impacting the nature of our work, how we do it, and the skills we need to be successful.

Present these five drivers to the participants. By a show of hands, have everyone provide their quick, immediate reaction to the following question:

Which driver is the most interesting or relevant to your work?

In small groups, go through the ideas and curiosities on the flipchart. Using worksheet #2 (see the Appendix for a printable version), determine which drivers relate to each theme or category that was identified. Rate the relevance of the drivers to the themes/categories using a 1-5 scale. The most relevant driver should receive a five, and the least relevant drivers should receive a one.

During this group work, consider the following questions:

1. Do different members of your group understand the same curiosity differently?
2. Which driver receives the lowest total score? The highest? Why do you think this is?
3. How does the relevance of the drivers compare with the driver that you initially found most interesting or relevant to your work?

Come back together. Have each group summarize how they ranked the themes/categories according to the five drivers. During this group discussion, consider the following:

- Which drivers were ranked the most and least relevant overall (by adding up their total scores)?
- Why are these drivers viewed as the most/least relevant?
- Are there any significantly different perspectives among participants?
- Why are different themes or drivers perceived differently?

Note for the Facilitator

At the end of the conversation, summarize the discussions and any "a-ha" moments that took place.

In all likelihood, the ideas that were discussed did not fall neatly into any one driver. A key takeaway from this activity is that the drivers should be used to challenge predictions about the future, as well as how we should react to them.

Whenever we learn about a new prediction or topic of discussion related to the Future of Work and the changes it will bring, think critically and ask questions. For example:

- What will it mean for different demographics? Who will benefit? Who might be left behind?
- How can workers take ownership over this change?
- What traditional approach to organizing work, income, and benefits might be threatened? What new opportunities might emerge from these structures?
- Who's offering a new way for products and services to reach the people that want and/or need them?
- How is technology impacting the world of work as we currently understand it?

Activity Two: Experiment-in-a-Box

Estimated allotted time: 30 minutes

For this activity, divide into teams of three and use worksheet #3 (pictured below; see the Appendix for a printable version and two samples) to create an experiment that you could conduct on the job.

The goal of this activity is to explore how you can shift your understandings of your work, your clients' experiences, and/or the way your workplace is structured so that you're moving closer to the future that you want to see.

First—

recall a time when your attitude and behaviour shifted and you found yourself positively changing the way you saw yourself, your work, your clients' potential, and your life. This is a thought experiment to get you thinking about the power you have to affect change, no matter how big or small.

- What was the journey?
- Who was responsible or contributed to the shift?
- What did they say and/or do?
- What did you say and/or do?
- What, specifically, caused the shift?

Second—

using the sense of accomplishment from that memory, identify a theme or driver that you and your team would like to experiment with on the job. Based on the discussion so far, you should agree on a specific question about your chosen topic, and start thinking in broad strokes about how it could affect your work, clients, and the sector as a whole now and in the future.

Third—

with this specific question in mind, list what could happen if your fears about the future come to pass.

Fourth—

with this specific question in mind, list what could happen if your dreams about the future come true.

Fifth—

complete the worksheet fully.

Sixth—

As a team, decide if you have all of the resources that you need (time, contacts, information, money, access, skills, etc.) to complete this experiment. If you don't, draw a new "pre-experiment" map that has "how will we get the resources we need to be ready to answer our initial question" as the question/curiosity, and go from there.

> Note for the Facilitator
> At the end of the conversation, collect the worksheets from each team and submit them to Challenge Factory (taryn@challengefactory.ca).

Appendix

Worksheets

Worksheet #1 24
Worksheet #2 25
Worksheet #3 26
       Sample 1 28
       Sample 2 30
Additional Resources 32

Worksheet #1

Conversation A: To Dread and to Dream the Future of Work

Activity Four: Our Colleagues Coast to Coast to Coast

Watch the video (see page 5 for the URL). Complete this worksheet independently before coming together to discuss your answers as a group.

1. What are your first reactions to the video?	
2. What surprised you?	
3. What didn't surprise you?	
4. What did the video confirm or reinforce in your current thinking?	
5. How did the video change your current understanding of the following topics:	
a. Future of Work	
b. The career development and employment services sector	
c. This moment in time as it relates to your work, role, and opportunities	
d. Your personal motivation	

Worksheet #2

Conversation C: Taking Action to Shape the Future of Work

Activity One: From Curiosity to Framework – Five Future of Work Drivers

Complete this worksheet in small groups. Consider the following questions as you work through it.

1. Do different members of your group understand the same curiosity differently?
2. Which driver receives the lowest total score? The highest? Why do you think this is?
3. How does the relevance of the drivers compare with the driver that you initially found most interesting or relevant to your work?

Scale: 1 – 5   1 = the driver has the least relevance to your theme/curiosity
          5 = the driver has the most relevance to your theme/curiosity

Theme or Curiosity	Relevance of the Five Future of Work Drivers				
	Demographics and Longevity	Career Ownership	Freelance/Gig Economy	Platform-based Models	AI and Robotics
Ex. Education that is future-proof	2	5	1	4	4
Ex. Automation of job search and recruitment	2	3	1	4	5
Total					

Worksheet #3

Conversation C: Taking Action to Shape the Future of Work

Activity Two: Experiment-in-a-Box

In teams of three, use this worksheet to create a Future of Work experiment that you could conduct on the job.

1. Theme or driver:

2. Our question/curiosity:

3. Our hypothesis:

4. Steps to testing the hypothesis:

5. How long will it take to complete these steps?

6. Who or what do we want to positively influence?

7. How will we know if our experiment has made an impact on this person/group/process/situation?

8. What resources do we need to conduct this experiment?

9. Signs that we are giving into our fears:

10. How will we take care of each other, recognise when we lose faith, restore and regenerate our beliefs, and enjoy the experiment?

Worksheet #3 – Sample 1

Conversation C: Taking Action to Shape the Future of Work

Activity Two: Experiment-in-a-Box

1. Theme or driver:
Remote work/freelance economy
2. Our question/curiosity:
How can low-skilled workers in remote geographies participate in the freelance economy?
3. Our hypothesis:
Our clients are interested in remote work but don't have the skills or technology to participate.
4. Steps to testing the hypothesis: • We need to learn more about remote work and employers who hire remote workers. • We need to learn what our clients believe to be true about remote work. • We need to learn if our clients use technology for non-work-related remote activities (e.g., keeping in touch with family, being part of community events, etc.). This will allow us to evaluate if they have hidden skills that they may not realize. • We need to learn what support our clients would need to shift from manufacturing/service sector employees to freelancers.
5. How long will it take to complete these steps?
This experiment is about testing an assumption we have about remote work. We should be able to gain a better understanding of what is happening and what our clients believe to be true within the next eight weeks.
6. Who or what do we want to positively influence? • Ourselves – we want to be more openminded and understanding about currently hidden opportunities. • Our clients – we want our clients to be more openminded and understanding about currently hidden opportunities. • Our supervisors – we want our supervisors to be able to access training, resources, and support to help clients pursue non-traditional means of employment.

7. How will we know if our experiment has made an impact on this person/group/process/situation?

- Ourselves – we will know more about how remote work options fit into the employment landscape that we want to be part of creating.
- Our Clients – we will know more about how much our clients know about remote work, their relevant skillsets, and what support they need if they are going to consider these options.
- Our supervisors – we will be able to spend time with clients learning and sharing remote work options without it negatively impacting our metrics, which is a priority to our supervisors.

8. What resources do we need to conduct this experiment?

- Reliable information from a variety of sources to inform us about what is happening in the world of remote work and freelancing for low-skilled workers and workers in remote geographies.
- Time to explore the perceptions and views of existing clients.
- Time to discuss this experiment as a team (i.e., time for productive and creative collaboration).
- … [list all resources, big and small]

9. Signs that we are giving into our fears:

- We end up talking to each other about the barriers facing this experiment rather than what we want to accomplish (pessimistic discussion of funding/reporting requirements, time limitations, etc.).
- We use the challenges that one or some of our clients are facing as the unavoidable reality of how all our clients will experience employment barriers if we try to experiment with remote work/freelance economy.

10. How will we take care of each other, recognise when we lose faith, restore and regenerate our beliefs, and enjoy the experiment?

- Remember that we're shaping the future – and that it's difficult! Come up with a word or phrase that captures this thought, and say it to each other whenever necessary.
- Share one success story or exchange that has happened recently that left us grateful, hopeful, or curious.
- Find one news article or resource about remote work or the freelance economy that is intriguing and share it with the team.

Worksheet #3 – Sample 2

Conversation C: Taking Action to Shape the Future of Work

Activity Two: Experiment-in-a-Box

1. Theme or driver: The importance of employment services
2. Our question/curiosity: Can we get other services in our agency to look to employment services as leaders in future-focused discussions?
3. Our hypothesis: Our expertise and work is not well understood by our board and colleagues. If we use tools like this conversation, we can shape the future of our services together and make all our work (and our agency as a whole) more productive and impactful.
4. Steps to testing the hypothesis: • Become activators and facilitators that will take this conversation to our colleagues.   • Share employment services resources and become a source of good information.   • Seek a formal role (such as "employment services representative") to lead the agency through new thinking as part of business planning.
5. How long will it take to complete these steps?   We will train ourselves to become activators and facilitators over the next two months, using our skills, voices, and resources during this year's business planning period in August.
6. Who or what do we want to positively influence?   • Ourselves – we want to prove to ourselves that we are experts in this field.   • Our colleagues and board – we want our colleagues and board to have access to internal, innovative resources and expert voices about the importance of employment services so that they can gain a better understanding.
7. How will we know if our experiment has made an impact on this person/group/process/situation?   • Our efforts are recognized and given buy-in by our colleagues and board.   • We are able to present our ideas about the importance of employment services in both informal and formal settings within the agency   • Our voices are included in this year's business planning period in August.

- Our voices lead to action by our colleagues and board (for example, they ask for follow-up, additional resources, or more of our perspectives on the importance of employment services).

8. What resources do we need to conduct this experiment?

- An understanding of how to navigate our agency's structures
- An outreach plan to implement
- Support from our immediate supervisor(s)
- Time to discuss this experiment as a team (i.e., time for productive and creative collaboration)
- ... [list all resources, big and small]

9. Signs that we are giving into our fears:

- After our experiment planning, we fail to put it into action because it just seems like too much work.
- We receive an initial lackluster response from other services in our agency and immediately decide this experiment is not worth pursuing anymore.
- We start to question whether we are the best voices, activators, and facilitators for this type of experiment.

10. How will we take care of each other, recognise when we lose faith, restore and regenerate our beliefs, and enjoy the experiment?

- Remember that shaping the future is a lot of work – but it's incredibly important and very much worthwhile in the long run. If we don't put in the work today, then tomorrow will see us living and working in a future that doesn't serve us or our clients.
- Turn to each other for team support and resilience. Stay optimistic, try again, and forge ahead.
- Reflect on the positive impact we've had on our past clients, and the knowledge we've gained through our training, experience, and hard work. We'll use this to remind ourselves that our expertise in this sector—and in our agency—is real, valid, and powerful.

Additional Resources

Analysis

Deloitte: Future of Work – Disruption lies ahead

Future Skills Centre: The Future of Work in Canada – What we need to know about our ecosystem

Organization for Economic Cooperation and Development (OECD): What is the Future of Work?

Initiatives

Ontario Non-Profit Network: Decent Work Project

World Economic Forum: Preparing for the Future of Work

Literature Searches

CERIC: Future of Work Literature Search

Labour Market Information Council (LMIC): The Now of Work Annotated Bibliography

Magazines

CareerWise by CERIC

The New York Times Magazine: Future of Work, Annual Issue

Videos and Podcasts

Challenge Factory: National Conversation on the Future of Work

The Atlantic: Future of Work: Leaping into the 2020s

TED Talks: Future of Work

McKinsey Global Institute: The New World of Work (eight-part podcast series)

www.ingramcontent.com/pod-product-compliance
Lightning Source LLC
Chambersburg PA
CBHW081423080526
44589CB00016B/2646